Quotes

Of

The

Royal Family

Collection of quotations said by royal family including Queen Elizabeth II, Prince Charles, Prince Philip, Princess Diana, Prince Harry, Prince William, Kate Middleton, Prince Andrew, and Queen Victoria

Table Of Content

Terms Of Use Agreement

Every effort had been made to fulfill requirements with regard to reproducing copyrighted material. The author and the publisher will be glad to certify any omissions at the earliest opportunity.

Disclaimer

The author and the publisher have used their best efforts in preparing this book. The author and the publisher make no representation or warranties with respect to the accuracy, fitness, applicability, or completeness of the contents of this work and specifically disclaim all warranties, including without limitation warranties of fitness for a particular purpose. This work is sold with the understanding that author and the publisher is not engaged in rendering legal, or any other professional services.

The information contained in this book is strictly for educational purposes. Therefore, if you wish to apply ideas contained within this book, you are taking full responsibility for your actions. The author and the publisher disclaim any warranties (express or implied), merchantability, or fitness for any particular purpose. The

Royal Family Quotes

When I appear in public people expect me to neigh, grind my teeth, paw the ground and swish my tail — none of which is easy.
— Princess Anne

Get me a beer. I don't care what kind it is, just get me a beer!
— Prince Philip when asked what he wanted at a dinner

William had to do his hair!
 — Duchess Kate on why they were late to an event

Father told me that if I ever met a lady in a dress like yours, I must look her straight in the eyes.
— Prince Charles to a beauty queen

When a man opens a car door for his wife, it's either a new car or a new wife.
— Prince Philip

Golf seems to be an arduous way to go for a walk. I prefer to take the dogs out.

— Princess Anne

British women can't cook.
— Prince Philip in a conversation to female cooks

I know I have the body of a weak, feeble woman; but I have the heart and stomach of a king, and of a king of England too...I myself will take up arms, I myself will be your general, judge, and re warder of every one of your virtues in the field.
– Elizabeth I, Speech to the Troops at Tilbury.

When I'm dead that boy will ruin himself within 12 months
– George V on his son, who became Edward VIII. Edward abdicated in the first year of his reign to marry divorcee Wallis Simpson.

Nothing that can be said can begin to take away the anguish and the pain of these moments. Grief is the price we pay for love.
– Elizabeth II in a message to the USA after 9/11.

I don't care what kind it is, just get me a beer!
– Prince Philip, after being offered wine in Rome in 2000.

I'm glad we've been bombed. It makes me feel I can look the East End in the face.
– The Queen Mother in 1940 after Buckingham Palace had been bombed.

I go from a corruptible to an incorruptible crown, where no disturbance can be, no disturbance in the world.
– Charles I on the scaffold just before his execution in 1649.

It was with some emotion...that I beheld Albert—who is beautiful.
– Victoria, on meeting Prince Albert, her future husband at the time.

I may be uninspiring, but I'll be damned if I'm an alien!
– George V after hearing that HG Wells called his court 'alien and uninspiring'.

My father was frightened of his mother; I was frightened
of my father, and I am damned well going to see to it
that my children are frightened of me.
– George V on discipline of his children.

I declare before you all that my whole life, whether it be
long or short, shall be devoted to your service and the
service of our great Imperial family to which we all
belong.
– Elizabeth II, 21st birthday speech, committing herself
to her then future role as Sovereign of the United
Kingdom.

I cannot lead you into battle, I do not give you laws or
administer justice but I can do something else, I can give
you my heart and my devotion to these old islands and
to all the peoples of our brotherhood of nations.
– Elizabeth II, 1957 Christmas Broadcast to the nation.

All these questions about do you want to be king? It's not
a question of wanting to be, it's something I was born
into and it's my duty, wanting is not the right word. But

those stories about me not wanting to be king are all wrong.
— Prince William, 21st birthday interview with the Press Association.

You are a pest, by the very nature of that camera in your hand.
– Princess Anne.

I really hope I can make a difference, even in the smallest way. I am looking forward to helping as much as I can.
– The Duchess of Cambridge post-engagement interview.

The highest of distinctions is service to others.
– George VI.

I learned the way a monkey learns — by watching its parents.
— Prince Charles

The man who invented the red carpet needed his head examined.
— Prince Philip

I have to be seen to be believed.
— Queen Elizabeth

To be honest, dinner conversations were the worst bit about being a child and listening to the boring people around me.
— Prince Harry

Like all the best families, we have our share of eccentricities, of impetuous and wayward youngsters and of family disagreements.
— Queen Elizabeth

Young people are the same as they always were. They are just as ignorant. — Prince Philip

As I learned from growing up, you don't mess with your grandmother.
— Prince William

I never see any home cooking — all I get is fancy stuff.
— Prince Philip

Quotes Of Queen Elizabeth II

I declare before you all that my whole life, whether it be long or short, shall be devoted to your service and the service of our great imperial family to which we all belong."
— Queen Elizabeth II

1992 is not a year I shall look back on with undiluted pleasure. In the words of one of my more sympathetic correspondents, it has turned out to be an 'annus horribles'".
— Queen Elizabeth II

No one who knew Diana will ever forget her. Millions of others who never met her, but felt they knew her, will remember her. I, for one, believe there are lessons to be drawn from her life and from the extraordinary and moving reaction to her death. I share in your determination to cherish her memory."
— Queen Elizabeth II

When life seems hard, the courageous do not lie down and accept defeat; instead, they are all the more determined to struggle for a better future."
— Queen Elizabeth II

Like all the best families, we have our share of eccentricities, of impetuous and wayward youngsters and of family disagreements."
— Queen Elizabeth II

In remembering the appalling suffering of war on both sides, we recognise how precious is the peace we have built in Europe since 1945.
— Queen Elizabeth II

I have to be seen to be believed.
— Queen Elizabeth II

The world is not the most pleasant place. Eventually your parents leave you and nobody is going to go out of their way to protect you unconditionally. You need to learn to stand up for yourself and what you believe and sometimes, pardon my language, kick some ass.
— Queen Elizabeth II

I know of no single formula for success. But over the years I have observed that some attributes of leadership are universal and are often about finding ways of encouraging people to combine their efforts, their talents, their insights, their enthusiasm and their inspiration to work together.
— Queen Elizabeth II

When life seems hard, the courageous do not lie down and accept defeat; instead, they are all the more determined to struggle for a better future.
— Queen Elizabeth II

It has turned out to be an annus horribilis.
— Queen Elizabeth II

Good memories are our second chance at happiness.
— Queen Elizabeth II

I don't like to badmouth people. But I'm the head of a monarchy that began in the ninth century, and I'm apparently more modern than Chris Christie. Look, I know he has to appeal to the crazy right-wingers in his

party, but the fact is, he's not as forward-thinking as an eighty-seven-year-old lady who wears a crown on her head. It's pathetic.
— Queen Elizabeth II

They are not royal. They just happen to have me as their aunt.
— Queen Elizabeth II

Therefore I am sure that this, my Coronation, is not the symbol of a power and a splendor that are gone but a declaration of our hopes for the future, and for the years I may, by God's Grace and Mercy, be given to reign and serve you as your Queen.
— Queen Elizabeth II

I believe that there is a great fear in our generation of being labeled as priggish.
— Queen Elizabeth II

It has been women who have breathed gentleness and care into the hard progress of humankind.
— Queen Elizabeth II

Cowards falter, but danger is often overcome by those who nobly dare.
— Queen Elizabeth II

It's all to do with the training: you can do a lot if you're properly trained.
— Queen Elizabeth II

Grief is the price we pay for love.
— Queen Elizabeth II

[On being criticized for her serious expression:] I simply ache from smiling. Why are women expected to beam all the time? It's unfair. If a man looks solemn, it's automatically assumed he's a serious person, not a miserable one.
— Queen Elizabeth II

Family does not necessarily mean blood relatives but often a description of a community, organisation or nation
— Queen Elizabeth II

True patriotism doesn't exclude an understanding of the patriotism of others.
— Queen Elizabeth II

Football's a difficult business and aren't they prima donnas. But it's a wonderful game.
— Queen Elizabeth II

The lessons from the peace process are clear; whatever life throws at us, our individual responses will be all the stronger for working together and sharing the load.
— Queen Elizabeth II

For me, heaven is likely to be a bit of a come-down.
— Queen Elizabeth II

Experience shows that great enterprises seldom end with a tidy and satisfactory flourish. Together, we are doing our best to re-establish peace and civil order in the Gulf region, and to help those members of civil and ethnic minorities who continue to suffer through no fault of their own. If we succeed, our military success will have achieved its true objective.
— Queen Elizabeth II

My husband has quite simply been my strength and stay all these years, and I owe him a debt greater than he would ever claim.
— Queen Elizabeth II

[Before each of numerous portrait sittings:]
Now then, with teeth or without?
— Queen Elizabeth II

There are long periods when life seems a small, dull round, a petty business with no point, and then suddenly we are caught up in some great event which gives us a glimpse of the solid and durable foundations of our existence.
— Queen Elizabeth II

I have behind me not only the splendid traditions and the annals of more than a thousand years but the living strength and majesty of the Commonwealth and Empire; of societies old and new; of lands and races different in history and origins but all, by God's Will, united in spirit and in aim.
— Queen Elizabeth II

Work is the rent you pay for the room you occupy on earth.

— Queen Elizabeth II

For Christians, as for all people of faith, reflection, meditation and prayer help us to renew ourselves in God's love, as we strive daily to become better people. The Christmas message shows us that this love is for everyone. There is no one beyond its reach.

— Queen Elizabeth II

Let us not take ourselves too seriously. None of us has a monopoly on wisdom.

— Queen Elizabeth II

[To the suggestion that Great Britain might someday want a Republic:] We'll go quietly.

— Queen Elizabeth II

We lost the American colonies because we lacked the statesmanship to know the right time and the manner of yielding what is impossible to keep.

— Queen Elizabeth II

[On the 1982 intruder into her bedroom:] I realized immediately that it wasn't a servant because they don't slam doors.
— Queen Elizabeth II

This new power, which has proved itself to be such a terrifying weapon of destruction, is harnessed for the first time for the common good of our community.
— Queen Elizabeth II

This thing called love, it cries like a baby in a cradle all night. It swings, it jives, it shakes all over like a jelly fish. I kinda like it.
— Queen Elizabeth II

We have all felt those emotions in these last few days. So what I say to you now, as your queen and as a grandmother, I say from my heart.
— Queen Elizabeth II

Like all the best families, we have our share of eccentricities, of impetuous and wayward youngsters and of family disagreements.
— Queen Elizabeth II

The upward course of a nation's history is due in the long run to the soundness of heart of its average men and women
— Queen Elizabeth II

At Christmas, I am always struck by how the spirit of togetherness lies also at the heart of the Christmas story. A young mother and a dutiful father with their baby were joined by poor shepherds and visitors from afar. They came with their gifts to worship the Christ child.
— Queen Elizabeth II

I should like to be a horse.
— Queen Elizabeth II

To all those who have suffered as a consequence of our troubled past I extend my sincere thoughts and deep sympathy. With the benefit of historical hindsight we can all see things which we would wish had been done differently or not at all.
— Queen Elizabeth II

We all need to get the balance right between action and reflection. With so many distractions, it is easy to forget to pause and take stock.
— Queen Elizabeth II

The events that I have attended to mark my Diamond Jubilee have been a humbling experience. It has touched me deeply to see so many thousands of families, neighbors and friends celebrating together in such a happy atmosphere.
— Queen Elizabeth II

To what greater inspiration and counsel can we turn than to the imperishable truth to be found in this treasure house, the Bible?
— Queen Elizabeth II

It has perhaps always been the case that the waging of peace is the hardest form of leadership of all.
— Queen Elizabeth II

It is as queen of Canada that I am here. Queen of Canada and all Canadians, not just one or two ancestral strains.

— Queen Elizabeth II

Quotes Of Prince Charles

I have not the slightest hesitation in making the observation that much of British management doesn't seem to understand the importance of the human factor.
— Prince Charles

I thought the British people were supposed to be compassionate. I don't see much of it.
— Prince Charles

Relationships with fathers can be such complex ones … So often, I suppose one must long to have got on better or to have been able to talk freely about the things that matter deeply, but one was too inhibited to discuss.
— Prince Charles

Any excuse to escape from Cambridge and plod across ploughed fields instead of stagnating in lecture rooms is enormously welcome.
— Prince Charles

The trouble is I always feel that unless I rush about doing things and trying to help furiously I will not (and the monarchy will not) be seen to be relevant and I will be considered a mere playboy!
— Prince Charles

This was one of those special occasions when I could actually feel the inner appreciation of the beauty of the moment passing like an electric current through the brush in my hand.
— Prince Charles

As technology advances at an alarming pace, the place of drawing remains as valid as ever in the creation of art and architecture.
— Prince Charles

It's funny, the influence that women can have on getting us men sorted out is enormous. I don't know why it is, but so often men have to come up against a brick wall before they suddenly realize they have to alter their way of operating in order to improve their health
— Prince Charles

I do have some understanding I think, a little, of what people go through with these horrors.
— Prince Charles

A renaissance of mutton won't change the world but it just might, might make the difference between [farmers'] survival and disappearance and that, ladies and gentlemen, is enough for me.
— Prince Charles

Addressing all these threats to our long-term survival will clearly require a massive and coordinated response from all sectors of society and in all nations.
— Prince Charles

Somehow, we have to find the courage to re-assert the once commonplace belief that human beings have a duty to act as the stewards of creation.
— Prince Charles

Both our nations have been united by grief and strengthened by the support we have given each other.
— Prince Charles

Our hearts go out to you today as they did on that dreadful today.
— Prince Charles

If you make everything over efficient, you suck out, it seems to me, every last drop of what, up to now, has been known as culture.
— Prince Charles

Quotes of Prince Philip

To a car park attendant who didn't recognise him in 1997, he snapped: You bloody silly fool!
— Prince Philip

To Simon Kelner, republican editor of The Independent, at Windsor Castle reception: What are you doing here? I was invited, sir. Philip: Well, you didn't have to come.
— Prince Philip

To female sea cadet last year: Do you work in a strip club?
— Prince Philip

To expats in Abu Dhabi last year: Are you running away from something?
— Prince Philip

After accepting a conservation award in Thailand in 1991: Your country is one of the most notorious centres of trading in endangered species.
— Prince Philip

At a project to protect turtle doves in Anguilla in 1965, he said: Cats kill far more birds than men. Why don't you have a slogan: 'Kill a cat and save a bird?'
— Prince Philip

To multi-ethnic Britain's Got Talent 2009 winners Diversity: Are you all one family?
— Prince Philip

To President of Nigeria, who was in national dress, 2003: You look like you're ready for bed!
— Prince Philip

His description of Beijing, during a visit there in 1986: Ghastly.
— Prince Philip

At Hertfordshire University, 2003: During the Blitz, a lot of shops had their windows blown in and put up notices saying, 'More open than usual'. I now declare this place more open than usual.
— Prince Philip

To deaf children by steel band, 2000: Deaf? If you're near there, no wonder you are deaf.

— Prince Philip

To a tourist in Budapest in 1993: You can't have been here long, you haven't got a pot belly.

— Prince Philip

To a British trekker in Papua New Guinea, 1998: You managed not to get eaten then?

— Prince Philip

His verdict on Stoke-on-Trent, during a visit in 1997: Ghastly.

— Prince Philip

To Atul Patel at reception for influential Indians, 2009: There's a lot of your family in tonight.

— Prince Philip

Peering at a fuse box in a Scottish factory, he said: It looks as though it was put in by an Indian. He later backtracked: I meant to say cowboys.

— Prince Philip

To Lockerbie residents after plane bombing, 1993: People say after a fire it's water damage that's the worst. We're still drying out Windsor Castle.
— Prince Philip

In Canada in 1976: We don't come here for our health.
— Prince Philip

I never see any home cooking – all I get is fancy stuff. 1987
— Prince Philip

On the Duke of York's house, 1986: It looks like a tart's bedroom.
— Prince Philip

Using Hitler's title to address German chancellor Helmut Kohl in 1997, he called him: Reichskanzler.
— Prince Philip

We go into the red next year... I shall have to give up polo. 1969.
— Prince Philip

At party in 2004: Bugger the table plan, give me my dinner!

— Prince Philip

To a woman solicitor, 1987: I thought it was against the law for a woman to solicit.

— Prince Philip

To a civil servant, 1970: You're just a silly little Whitehall twit: you don't trust me and I don't trust you.

— Prince Philip

On the 1981 recession: A few years ago, everybody was saying we must have more leisure, everyone's working too much. Now everybody's got more leisure time they're complaining they're unemployed. People don't seem to make up their minds what they want.

— Prince Philip

On the new £18 million British Embassy in Berlin in 2000: It's a vast waste of space.

— Prince Philip

After Dunblane massacre, 1996: If a cricketer suddenly decided to go into a school and batter a lot of people to death with a cricket bat, are you going to ban cricket bats?
— Prince Philip

To the Aircraft Research Association in 2002: If you travel as much as we do, you appreciate the improvements in aircraft design of less noise and more comfort – provided you don't travel in something called economy class, which sounds ghastly.
— Prince Philip

On stress counselling for servicemen in 1995: We didn't have counsellors rushing around every time somebody let off a gun. You just got on with it!
— Prince Philip

On Tom Jones, 1969: It's difficult to see how it's possible to become immensely valuable by singing what are the most hideous songs.
— Prince Philip

To the Scottish WI in 1961: British women can't cook.
— Prince Philip

To the Paraguayan dictator General Stroessner: It's a pleasure to be in a country that isn't ruled by its people.
— Prince Philip

To Cayman Islanders: Aren't most of you descended from pirates?
— Prince Philip

To Scottish driving instructor, 1995: How do you keep the natives off the booze long enough to pass the test?
— Prince Philip

At a WF meeting in 1986: If it has four legs and it's not a chair, if it's got two wings and it flies but is not an aeroplane and if it swims and it's not a submarine, the Cantonese will eat it.
— Prince Philip

You ARE a woman, aren't you? Kenya, 1984.
— Prince Philip

A VIP at a local airport asked HRH: What was your flight, like, Your Royal Highness? Philip: Have you ever flown in a plane? VIP: Oh yes, sir, many times. Well, said Philip, it was just like that.
— Prince Philip

On Ethiopian art, 1965: It looks like the kind of thing my daughter would bring back from school art lessons.
— Prince Philip

To a fashion writer in 1993: You're not wearing mink knickers,are you?
— Prince Philip

To Susan Edwards and her guide dog in 2002: They have eating dogs for the anorexic now.
— Prince Philip

When offered wine in Rome in 2000, he snapped: I don't care what kind it is, just get me a beer!
— Prince Philip

I'd like to go to Russia very much – although the bastards murdered half my family.
— Prince Philip

At City Hall in 2002: If we could just stop the tourism, we could stop the congestion.
— Prince Philip

On seeing a piezometer water gauge in Australia: A pissometer?
— Prince Philip

You have mosquitoes. I have the Press. To matron of Caribbean hospital, 1966.
— Prince Philip

At a Bangladeshi youth club in 2002:So who's on drugs here?... HE looks as if he's on drugs.
— Prince Philip

To a children's band in Australia in 2002: You were playing your instruments? Or do you have tape recorders under your seats?
— Prince Philip

At Duke of Edinburgh Awards scheme, 2006. Young people are the same as they always were. Just as ignorant.

— Prince Philip

On how difficult it is in Britain to get rich: What about Tom Jones? He's made a million and he's a bloody awful singer.

— Prince Philip

To Elton John on his gold Aston Martin in 2001: Oh, it's you that owns that ghastly car, is it?

— Prince Philip

At an engineering school closed so he could officially open it, 2005: It doesn't look like much work goes on at this university.

— Prince Philip

To Aboriginal leader William Brin, Queensland, 2002: Do you still throw spears at each film other?

— Prince Philip

At a Scottish fish farm: Oh! You're the people ruining the rivers.

— Prince Philip

After a breakfast of bacon, eggs, smoked salmon, kedgeree, croissants and pain au chocolat – from Gallic chef Regis Crépy, 2002: The French don't know how to cook breakfast.

— Prince Philip

To schoolboy who invited the Queen to Romford, Essex, 2003: Ah, you're the one who wrote the letter. So you can write then?

— Prince Philip

To black politician Lord Taylor of Warwick, 1999: And what exotic part of the world do you come from?

— Prince Philip

To parents at a previously struggling Sheffield school, 2003: Were you here in the bad old days? ... That's why you can't read and write then!

— Prince Philip

To Andrew Adams, 13, in 1998: You could do with losing a little bit of weight.
— Prince Philip

Where's the Southern Comfort? When presented with a hamper of goods by US ambassador, 1999.
— Prince Philip

To editor of downmarket tabloid: Where are you from? The S*n, sir. Philip: Oh, no . . . one can't tell from the outside.
— Prince Philip

Turning down food, 2000: No, I'd probably end up spitting it out over everybody.
— Prince Philip

Asking Cate Blanchett to fix his DVD player because she worked in the film industry, 2008: There's a cord sticking out of the back. Might you tell me where it goes?
— Prince Philip

People think there's a rigid class system here, but dukes have even been known to marry chorus girls. Some have even married Americans. 2000.
— Prince Philip

After hearing President Obama had had breakfast with leaders of the UK, China and Russia, 2010: Can you tell the difference between them?
— Prince Philip

On students from Brunei, 1998: I don't know how they're going to integrate in places like Glasgow and Sheffield.
— Prince Philip

On Princess Anne, 1970: If it doesn't fart or eat hay, she isn't interested.
— Prince Philip

To wheelchair-bound nursing-home resident, 2002: Do people trip over you?
— Prince Philip

Discussing tartan with the-Scottish Tory leader Annabel Goldie last year: That's a nice tie... Do you have any knickers in that material?
— Prince Philip

To a group of industrialists in 1961: I've never been noticeably reticent about talking on subjects about which I know nothing.
— Prince Philip

On a crocodile he shot in Gambia in 1957: It's not a very big one, but at least it's dead and it took an awful lot of killing!
— Prince Philip

On being made Chancellor of Edinburgh University in 1953: Only a Scotsman can really survive a Scottish education.
— Prince Philip

I must be the only person in Britain glad to see the back of that plane. He hated the noise Concorde made flying over Buckingham Palace, 2002
— Prince Philip

To a fashion designer, 2009: Well, you didn't design your beard too well, did you?
— Prince Philip

To the General Dental Council in 1960: Dontopedalogy is the science of opening your mouth and putting your foot in it, which I've practised for many years.
— Prince Philip

On stroking a koala in 1992: Oh no, I might catch some ghastly disease.
— Prince Philip

On marriage in 1997: You can take it from me the Queen has the quality of tolerance in abundance.
— Prince Philip

To schoolchildren in blood-red uniforms, 1998: It makes you all look like Dracula's daughters!
— Prince Philip

I don't think a prostitute is more moral than a wife, but they are doing the same thing. 1988.
— Prince Philip

To female Labour MPs in 2000: So this is feminist corner then.

— Prince Philip

On Nottingham Forest trophies in 1999: I suppose I'd get in trouble if I were to melt them down.

— Prince Philip

It's my custom to say something flattering to begin with so I shall be excused if I put my foot in it later on. 1956.

— Prince Philip

To a penniless student in 1998: Why don't you go and live in a hostel to save cash?

— Prince Philip

On robots colliding, Science Museum, 2000: They're not mating are they?

— Prince Philip

While stuck in a Heriot Watt University lift in 1958: This could only happen in a technical college.

— Prince Philip

To newsreader Michael Buerk, when told he knew about the Duke of Edinburgh's Gold Awards, 2004: That's more than you know about anything else then.
— Prince Philip

To a British student in China, 1986: If you stay here much longer, you'll go home with slitty eyes.
— Prince Philip

To journalist Caroline Wyatt, who asked if the Queen was enjoying a Paris trip, 2006: Damn fool question!
— Prince Philip

On smoke alarms to a woman who lost two sons in a fire, 1998: They're a damn nuisance - I've got one in my bathroom and every time I run my bath the steam sets it off.
— Prince Philip

Quotes of Princess Diana

Only do what your heart tells you.
— Princess Diana

Family is the most important thing in the world.
— Princess Diana

If you find someone you love in your life, then hang on to that love.
— Princess Diana

Carry out a random act of kindness, with no expectation of reward, safe in the knowledge that one day someone might do the same for you.
— Princess Diana

The biggest disease this day and age is that of people feeling unloved.
— Princess Diana

Everyone of us needs to show how much we care for each other and, in the process, care for ourselves.
— Princess Diana

Anywhere I see suffering, that is where I want to be, doing what I can.
— Princess Diana

Nothing brings me more happiness than trying to help the most vulnerable people in society. It is a goal and an essential part of my life - a kind of destiny. Whoever is in distress can call on me. I will come running wherever they are.
— Princess Diana

The greatest problem in the world today is intolerance. Everyone is so intolerant of each other.
— Princess Diana

There were three of us in this marriage, so it was a bit crowded.
— Princess Diana

I'd like to be a queen in people's hearts but I don't see myself being queen of this country.
— Princess Diana

What must it be like for a little boy to read that daddy never loved mummy?
— Princess Diana

I want to walk into a room, be it a hospital for the dying or a hospital for the sick children, and feel that I am needed. I want to do, not just to be.
— Princess Diana

I want my boys to have an understanding of people's emotions, their insecurities, people's distress, and their hopes and dreams.
— Princess Diana

HIV does not make people dangerous to know, so you can shake their hands and give them a hug: Heaven knows they need it.
— Princess Diana

They say it is better to be poor and happy than rich and miserable, but how about a compromise like moderately rich and just moody?
— Princess Diana

I like to be a free spirit. Some don't like that, but that's the way I am.

— Princess Diana

I think the biggest disease the world suffers from in this day and age is the disease of people feeling unloved. I know that I can give love for a minute, for half an hour, for a day, for a month, but I can give. I am very happy to do that, I want to do that.

— Princess Diana

Hugs can do great amounts of good - especially for children.

— Princess Diana

I'm as thick as a plank.

— Princess Diana

Life is just a journey.

— Princess Diana

Being a princess isn't all it's cracked up to be.

— Princess Diana

I knew what my job was; it was to go out and meet the people and love them.
— Princess Diana

I live for my sons. I would be lost without them.
— Princess Diana

I don't even know how to use a parking meter, let alone a phone box.
— Princess Diana

I don't want expensive gifts; I don't want to be bought. I have everything I want. I just want someone to be there for me, to make me feel safe and secure.
— Princess Diana

It's vital that the monarchy keeps in touch with the people. It's what I try and do.
— Princess Diana

People think that at the end of the day a man is the only answer. Actually, a fulfilling job is better for me.
— Princess Diana

You can't comfort the afflicted with afflicting the comfortable.
— Princess Diana

I don't go by the rule book... I lead from the heart, not the head.
— Princess Diana

When you are happy you can forgive a great deal.
— Princess Diana

I will fight for my children on any level so they can reach their potential as human beings and in their public duties.
— Princess Diana

I wear my heart on my sleeve.
— Princess Diana

Any sane person would have left long ago. But I cannot. I have my sons.
— Princess Diana

I'm aware that people I have loved and have died and are in the spirit world looking after me.
— Princess Diana

If men had to have babies, they would only ever have one each.
— Princess Diana

I think like any marriage, especially when you've had divorced parents like myself; you want to try even harder to make it work.
— Princess Diana

So many people supported me through my public life and I will never forget them.
— Princess Diana

The kindness and affection from the public have carried me through some of the most difficult periods, and always your love and affection have eased the journey.
Princess Diana

Prince Harry Quotes

Anyone who says they don't enjoy the Army is mad - you can spend a week hating it and the next week it could be the best thing in the world and the best job you could ever, ever wish for. It has got so much to offer.
— Prince Harry

I'm still very much a kid inside myself.
— Prince Harry

I've longed for kids since I was very, very young. And so... I'm waiting to find the right person, someone who's willing to take on the job.
— Prince Harry

You've got to give something back. You can't just sit there.
— Prince Harry

I've served my country.
— Prince Harry

Conversations with my mother, father, my grandparents, as I've grown up have obviously driven me towards wanting to try and make a difference as much as possible.

— Prince Harry

There's a lot of times that both myself and my brother wish, obviously, that we were just completely normal.

— Prince Harry

For me personally, as I said, I want to serve my country. I've done it once, and I'm still in the army, I feel as though I should get the opportunity to do it again.

— Prince Harry

I get a huge buzz from spending time with kids.

— Prince Harry

Once you're in the military, she means a lot more to you than just a grandmother. She is the queen. And then you suddenly, it's like start realizing, you know, wow, this is quite a big deal. And then you get goose bumps and then the rest of it.

— Prince Harry

To be honest dinner conversations was the worst bit about being a child and listening to the boring people around me.
— Prince Harry

You can imagine the kind of dinner parties I had to go to at a young age... pretty dull.
— Prince Harry

I've longed for kids since I was very, very young.
— Prince Harry

Prince William Quotes

My guiding principles in life are to be honest, genuine, thoughtful and caring.
— Prince William

I always remember having a healthy respect for my grandmother.
— Prince William

When the Queen says 'well done,' it means so much.
— Prince William

It's like a rugby team. If you're picking for the World Cup final, you're picking experience with youth. Everything is better off having that balance and that mix. I think that, especially, goes for the monarchy as well.
— Prince William

When I first met Kate I knew there was something very special about her. I knew there was possibly something that I wanted to explore there. We ended up being friends for a while and that just sort of was a good foundation. Because I do generally believe now that

being friends with one another is a massive advantage.
And It just went from there.
— Prince William

I hope I'm not a tourist attraction - I'm sure that they
come here really because St. Andrews is just amazing, a
beautiful place.
— Prince William

As any new parent knows, you're only too happy to show
off your new child and, you know, proclaim that he is the
best looking or the best everything.
— Prince William

I'm probably a bit of a cheeky grandson like my brother
as well. We both tend to take the mickey a bit much.
— Prince William

As I learned from growing up, you don't mess with your
grandmother.
— Prince William

I've had lots of kids come up and ask for my autograph, I've had a grandmother stop me and ask me if I know a good place to buy underwear.
— Prince William

There's been a lot of speculation about every single girl I'm with and it actually does quite irritate me after a while, more so because it's a complete pain for the girls.
— Prince William

I am as independent as I want to be, same as Catherine and Harry. We've all grown up differently to other generations and I very much feel if that I can do it myself, I want to do it myself.
— Prince William

People say it's not ambitious, but it is actually quite ambitious wanting to help people.
— Prince William

I have to say that I thought search-and-rescue duties over Snowdonia were physically and mentally

demanding, but looking after a 3-week-old baby is up there!
— Prince William

I think it's very important that you make your own decision about what you are. Therefore you're responsible for your actions, so you don't blame other people.
— Prince William

I'm always open for people saying I'm wrong because most of the time I am.
— Prince William

I'm reasonably headstrong about what I believe in, and what I go for, and I've got fantastic people around me who give me great support and advice.
— Prince William

Being a small boy it's very daunting seeing the Queen around and not really quite knowing what to talk about.
— Prince William

We'll sort of get over the marriage first and then maybe look at the kids. But obviously we want a family so we'll have to start thinking about that.
— Prince William

When I was younger and my parents used to always slap my hand if I was picking my nose or if I was running around screaming I was told to shut up.
— Prince William

No one is going to try to fill my mother's shoes, what she did was fantastic. It's about making your own future and your own destiny and Kate will do a very good job of that.
— Prince William

There's no pressure; like Kate said, it is about carving your own future. No one is going to try to fill my mother's shoes; what she did was fantastic. It's about making your own future and your own destiny, and Kate will do a very good job of that.
— Prince William

I'm still trying to decide. It's a really difficult one because I really enjoy my time in the Air Force. And I'd love to continue it. But the pressures of my other life are building. And fighting them off or balancing the two of them has proven quite difficult.
— Prince William

There are times where you can't do it yourself and the system takes over, or it's appropriate to do things differently. But I think driving your son and your wife away from hospital was really important to me.
— Prince William

I'm just very keen to have a family and both Catherine and I, you know, are looking forward to having a family in the future.
— Prince William

It's my mother's engagement ring so I thought it was quite nice because obviously she's not going to be around to share any of the fun and excitement of it all - this was my way of keeping her close to it all.
— Prince William

My guiding principles in life are to be honest, genuine, thoughtful and caring.
— Prince William

I always remember having a healthy respect for my grandmother.
— Prince William

When the Queen says 'well done,' it means so much.
— Prince William

It's like a rugby team. If you're picking for the World Cup final, you're picking experience with youth. Everything is better off having that balance and that mix. I think that, especially, goes for the monarchy as well.
— Prince William

When I first met Kate I knew there was something very special about her. I knew there was possibly something that I wanted to explore there. We ended up being friends for a while and that just sort of was a good foundation.

Because I do generally believe now that being friends with one another is a massive advantage. And It just went from there.
— Prince William

I hope I'm not a tourist attraction - I'm sure that they come here really because St. Andrews is just amazing, a beautiful place.
— Prince William

As any new parent knows, you're only too happy to show off your new child and, you know, proclaim that he is the best looking or the best everything.
— Prince William

I'm probably a bit of a cheeky grandson like my brother as well. We both tend to take the mickey a bit much.
— Prince William

As I learned from growing up, you don't mess with your grandmother.
— Prince William

I've had lots of kids come up and ask for my autograph, I've had a grandmother stop me and ask me if I know a good place to buy underwear.
— Prince William

There's been a lot of speculation about every single girl I'm with and it actually does quite irritate me after a while, more so because it's a complete pain for the girls.
— Prince William

I am as independent as I want to be, same as Catherine and Harry. We've all grown up differently to other generations and I very much feel if that I can do it myself, I want to do it myself.
— Prince William

People say it's not ambitious, but it is actually quite ambitious wanting to help people.
— Prince William

I have to say that I thought search-and-rescue duties over Snowdonia were physically and mentally

demanding, but looking after a 3-week-old baby is up there!
— Prince William

I think it's very important that you make your own decision about what you are. Therefore you're responsible for your actions, so you don't blame other people.
— Prince William

I'm always open for people saying I'm wrong because most of the time I am.
— Prince William

I'm reasonably headstrong about what I believe in, and what I go for, and I've got fantastic people around me who give me great support and advice.
— Prince William

Being a small boy it's very daunting seeing the Queen around and not really quite knowing what to talk about.
— Prince William

We'll sort of get over the marriage first and then maybe look at the kids. But obviously we want a family so we'll have to start thinking about that.
— Prince William

When I was younger and my parents used to always slap my hand if I was picking my nose or if I was running around screaming I was told to shut up.
— Prince William

No one is going to try to fill my mother's shoes, what she did was fantastic. It's about making your own future and your own destiny and Kate will do a very good job of that.
— Prince William

There's no pressure; like Kate said, it is about carving your own future. No one is going to try to fill my mother's shoes; what she did was fantastic. It's about making your own future and your own destiny, and Kate will do a very good job of that.
— Prince William

I'm still trying to decide. It's a really difficult one because I really enjoy my time in the Air Force. And I'd love to continue it. But the pressures of my other life are building. And fighting them off or balancing the two of them has proven quite difficult.

— Prince William

There are times where you can't do it yourself and the system takes over, or it's appropriate to do things differently. But I think driving your son and your wife away from hospital was really important to me.

— Prince William

I'm just very keen to have a family and both Catherine and I, you know, are looking forward to having a family in the future.

— Prince William

It's my mother's engagement ring so I thought it was quite nice because obviously she's not going to be around to share any of the fun and excitement of it all - this was my way of keeping her close to it all.

— Prince William

Kate Middleton Quotes

The attitudes towards mental health must change
— Kate Middleton

No one would feel embarrassed about seeking help for a child if they broke their arm and we really should be equally ready to support a child coping with emotional difficulties.
— Kate Middleton

Well I think if you really go out with someone for quite a long time you do get to know each other very, very well, you go through the good times, you go through the bad times. You know both personally, but also within a relationship as well.
— Kate Middleton

Yes, well I really hope I can make a difference, even in the smallest way. I am looking forward to helping as much as I can.
— Kate Middleton

By far the best dressing up outfit I ever had was a wonderful pair of clown dungarees, which my Granny made.
— Kate Middleton

A child's mental health is just as important as their physical health.
— Kate Middleton

Patriarchy's chief institution is the family. It is both a mirror of and a connection with the larger society; a patriarchal unit within a patriarchal whole.
— Kate Middleton

I think, the people around home are very supportive to us.
— Kate Middleton

I find doing speeches nerve wrecking.
— Kate Middleton

I don't know if I have a favorite color.
— Kate Middleton

I'm still very much Kate.

— Kate Middleton

I think I know I've been working very hard for the family business, sometimes those days are long days and I think if I know I'm working hard and pulling my weight, both working and playing hard at the same time, I think everyone who I work with can see I am there pulling my weight.

— Kate Middleton

I hope we will be able to have a happy family ourselves.

— Kate Middleton

No, I had the Levis guy on my wall, not a picture of William, sorry.

— Kate Middleton

I think at the time I wasn't very happy about it [marriage], but actually it made me a stronger person, you find out things about yourself that maybe you hadn't realized. I think you can get quite consumed by a relationship when you are younger and I really valued that time for me as well, although I didn't think it at the time.

— Kate Middleton

A huge amount still needs to be done. At the moment hundreds of children are still malnourished.

— Kate Middleton

I have learned that delivering the best possible palliative care to children is vital, providing children and their families with a place of support, care and enhancement at a time of great need is simply life-changing.

— Kate Middleton

Prince Andrew Quotes

I could have worse tags than 'Airmiles Andy' - although I don't know what they are.
— Prince Andrew

Today is reality. Yesterday is history.
— Prince Andrew

The Royal Family have always had an interest in a number of different areas of society. We are a part of society.
— Prince Andrew

It would not be a bad idea if bankers were to go and sit occasionally with politicians in their political surgeries, where they might get a sense of the injustice that some of the community feel about the banks.
— Prince Andrew

I've always been told I was extremely well-behaved as a kid.
— Prince Andrew

I'm in a privileged position and I'm going to do my utmost to use that privileged position on behalf of the U.K., its citizens, its businesses and people.
— Prince Andrew

I'll tell you where the injustice is. It's with the person earning £12,000 to £15,000-a-year who is being asked to be restrained by their business or employer. Yet the taxpayer has bailed out the banks, so why are they not showing restraint?
— Prince Andrew

I look at Canada like a second home.
— Prince Andrew

There is something about going to sea. A little bit of discipline, self-discipline and humility are required.
— Prince Andrew

In the U.K. we have the best geography teachers in the world.
— Prince Andrew

The Queen's intelligence network is a hell of a lot better than anyone's in this palace. Bar none. She knows everything. I don't know how she does it. And she sees everything.

— Prince Andrew

People say to me, Would you like to swap your life with me for 24 hours? Your life must be very strange. But of course I have not experienced any other life. It's not strange to me.

— Prince Andrew

It's slightly complicated for people to grasp the idea of a head of state in human form.

— Prince Andrew

When the question arose whether I, as a member of the royal family, should take part in active combat in the Falklands, there was no question in her mind, and it only took her two days to sort the issue.

— Prince Andrew

She is incredibly fit, but we remind staff that she's not just the monarch, but our mother.
— Prince Andrew

We're not allowed to play Monopoly at home. It gets too vicious.
— Prince Andrew

Quotes of Queen Victoria

Nothing will turn a man's home into a castle more quickly and effectively than a dachshund.
— Queen Victoria

Great events make me quiet and calm; it is only trifles that irritate my nerves.
— Queen Victoria

The important thing is not what they think of me, but what I think of them.
— Queen Victoria

We are not interested in the possibilities of defeat. They do not exist.
— Queen Victoria

We poor creatures are born for man's pleasure and amusement, and destined to go through endless sufferings and trials.
— Queen Victoria

Were women to "unsex" themselves by claiming equality with men, they would become the most hateful, heathen, and disgusting of beings and would surely perish without male protection.
— Queen Victoria

I positively think that ladies who are always enceinte quite disgusting; it is more like a rabbit or guinea-pig than anything else and really it is not very nice.
— Queen Victoria

Beware of artists, they mix with all classes of society and are therefore most dangerous.
— Queen Victoria

There is, however, another subject on which the Queen feels most strongly, and that is this horrible, brutalizing, un-Christian-like vivisection...It must really not be permitted. It is a disgrace to a civilized country.
— Queen Victoria

Just close your eyes—and think of England.
— Queen Victoria

[On alcohol:] Total abstinence is an impossibility and ...
it will not do to insist on it as a general practice ...
— Queen Victoria

Give my people plenty of beer, good beer, and cheap
beer, and you will have no revolution among them.
— Queen Victoria

I feel sure that no girl would go to the altar if she knew
all.
— Queen Victoria

I would venture to warn against too great intimacy with
artists as it is very seductive and a little dangerous.
— Queen Victoria

Bring me a cup of tea and the 'Times.'
— Queen Victoria

Lord Aberdeen was quite touched when I told him I was
so attached to the dear, dear Highlands and missed the
fine hills so much. There is a great peculiarity about the

Highlands and Highlanders; and they are such a chivalrous, fine, active people.
— Queen Victoria

The greatest maxim of all is that children should be brought up as simply and in as domestic a way as possible, and that (not interfering with their lessons) they should be as much as possible with their parents, and learn to place the greatest confidence in them in all things.
— Queen Victoria

That Book, the Bible, accounts for the supremacy of England. England has become great & happy by the knowledge of the true God through Jesus Christ.
— Queen Victoria

Oh! If those selfish men, who are the cause of all one's misery, only knew what their poor slaves go through! What suffering, what humiliation to the delicate feelings of a poor woman, above all a young one, especially with those nasty doctors.
— Queen Victoria

We placed the wreaths upon the splendid granite sarcophagus, and at its feet, and felt that only the earthly robe we loved so much was there. The pure, tender, loving spirit which loved us so tenderly, is above us - loving us, praying for us, and free from all suffering and woe - yes, that is a comfort, and that first birthday in another world must have been a far brighter one than any in this poor world below!
— Queen Victoria

I love peace and quiet, I hate politics and turmoil. We women are not made for governing, and if we are good women, we must dislike these masculine occupations.
— Queen Victoria

What you say of the pride of giving life to an immortal soul is very fine dear, but I own I cannot enter into that: I think much more of our being like a cow or a dog at such moments: when our poor nature becomes so very animal and unecstatic
— Queen Victoria

You will find as the children grow up that as a rule children are a bitter disappointment - their greatest

object being to do precisely what their parents do not wish and have anxiously tried to prevent.
— Queen Victoria

I am every day more convinced that we women, if we are to be good women, feminine and amiable and domestic, are not fitted to reign; at least it is they that drive themselves to the work which it entails.
— Queen Victoria

Since it has pleased Providence to place me in this station, I shall do my utmost to fulfil my duty towards my country; I am very young and perhaps in many, though not in all things, inexperienced, but I am sure that very few have more real good will and more real desire to do what is fit and right than I have.
— Queen Victoria

Oh, that peace may come.
— Queen Victoria

The poor fatherless baby of eight months is now the utterly broken-hearted and crushed widow of forty-two! My life as a happy one is ended! the world is gone for me! If I must live on (and I will do nothing to make me worse than I am), it is henceforth for our poor fatherless children - for my unhappy country, which has lost all in losing him - and in only doing what I know and feel he would wish.

— Queen Victoria

Affairs go on, and all will take some shape or other, but it keeps one in hot water all the time.

— Queen Victoria

Men never think, at least seldom think, what a hard task it is for us women to go through this very often. God's will be done, and if He decrees that we are to have a great number of children why we must try to bring them up as useful and exemplary members of society.

— Queen Victoria

We will not have failure - only success and new learning.

— Queen Victoria

I don't dislike babies, though I think very young ones rather disgusting.

— Queen Victoria

Being pregnant is an occupational hazard of being a wife.
— Queen Victoria

The danger to the country, to Europe, to her vast Empire, which is involved in having all these great interests entrusted to the shaking hand of an old, wild, and incomprehensible man of 82, is very great!
— Queen Victoria

Good Hock (Hochheimer) keeps off the Doc.
— Queen Victoria

The Government should take a firm, bold line. This delay - this uncertainty, by which, abroad, we are losing our prestige and our position, while Russia is advancing and will be before Constantinople in no time! Then the Government will be fearfully blamed and the Queen so humiliated that she thinks she would abdicate at once.
— Queen Victoria

I think people really marry far too much; it is such a lottery after all, and for a poor woman a very doubtful happiness.
— Queen Victoria

The Queen is most anxious to enlist everyone who can speak or write to join in checking this mad, wicked folly of Woman's Rights with all its attendant horrors on which her poor, feeble sex is bent, forgetting every sense of womanly feeling and propriety.
— Queen Victoria

[On same-sex marriage:] No woman would do that.
— Queen Victoria

She was such a beautiful and sweet creature... and so full of tricks.
— Queen Victoria

An ugly baby is a very nasty object - and the prettiest is frightful.
— Queen Victoria

The Queen is most anxious to enlist everyone in checking this mad, wicked folly of 'Women's Rights'. It is a subject which makes the Queen so furious that she cannot contain herself.
— Queen Victoria

My dearest dearest dear Albert sat on a footstool by my side and his excessive love and affection gave me feelings of heavenly love and happiness I never could have hoped to have felt before! He clasped me in his arms and we kissed each other again and again! His beauty... his sweetness and gentleness - really how can I ever be thankful enough to have such a husband! to be called names of tenderness, I have never yet heard used to me before - was bliss beyond belief! Oh! This was the happiest day of my life! May God help me to do my duty as I ought and be worthy of such blessings.
— Queen Victoria

Everybody grows but me.
— Queen Victoria

Being married gives one one's position like nothing else can.
— Queen Victoria

A marriage is no amusement but a solemn act, and generally a sad one.
— Queen Victoria

For a man to strike any women is most brutal, and I, as well as everyone else, think this far worse than any attempt to shoot, which, wicked as it is, is at least more comprehensible and more courageous.
— Queen Victoria

No civilization is complete which does not include the dumb and defenseless of God's creatures within the sphere of charity and mercy.
— Queen Victoria

Quotes About Royal Family

The interpretation of dreams is the royal road to a knowledge of the unconscious activities of the mind.
— Sigmund Freud

There is no royal road to geometry.
— Euclid

In the past, people were born royal. Nowadays, royalty comes from what you do.
— Gianni Versace

My life has been a tapestry of rich and royal hue, an everlasting vision of the ever changing view.
— Carole King

Winning the Royal Rumble is as big an accomplishment as anything.
— John Cena

There is no royal road to anything, one thing at a time, all things in succession. That which grows fast, withers as

rapidly. That which grows slowly, endures.
— Josiah Gilbert Holland

There's nothing so kingly as kindness, and nothing so royal as truth.
— Alice Cary

I just recently joined Twitter. It's very positive - I love all the accolades. If my ego is hurting, I can just open my Twitter account and see 'Oh, I love you! I love the show!' and it's great. I'm trying to find the balance between trying to be funny, being honest and just being a promoter as the guy on 'Royal Pains.'
— Mark Feuerstein

Jews have deep respect for the Queen and the royal family. We say a prayer for them every Sabbath in synagogue. We recite a special blessing on seeing the Queen.
— Jonathan Sacks

I love trying out different cuisines. In Delhi, I love Megu at the Leela, and TK's at the Hyatt. I also enjoy Khan

Chacha's rolls. In Mumbai, it's Royal China and Shiro.
And in Bangalore, I like the food at Bricklane.
— Virat Kohli

Being born into the Royal Family is like being born into a
mental asylum. Marrying into it is not something to be
taken lightly.
— John Lydon

The monarchy is foremost a business, and it's important
to them that the British public continue to finance the
excessive luxurious lifestyles of the now quite enormous,
wasteful and useless 'royal' family. I find it very sad.
— Steven Patrick Morrissey

There is something about — Prince William and Prince
Harry that brings real modernity to the British royal
family. They are also very open, human, and kind, and
this is what I have tried to capture in the pictures I have
taken of them as well as in my pictures of — Prince
William and Catherine.
— Mario Testino

There was no doubt that in the early and mid-eighties that many of us in broadsheet newspapers felt that we still had a responsibility to try to protect the Royal Family or if you like protect the Monarchy from the assaults of the media.
— Max Hastings

Teaching is the royal road to learning.
— Jessamyn West

I'd like to see a much more open Monarchy, myself. I used to think they were completely useless and we should get rid of them. I don't necessarily feel that way anymore. I'm still ambivalent, I still loathe the British class system, and the Royal family are the apex of the British class system.
— Helen Mirren

Economists, like royal children, are not punished for their errors.
— James Buchan

The Royal Navy of England hath ever been its greatest defense and ornament; it is its ancient and natural strength; the floating bulwark of the island.

— William Blackstone

Theatre outings are my favourite thing to spend money on. The most influential play I saw was 'Bent,' which starred Ian McKellen. And I loved the original performance of 'The Rocky Horror Show,' with Richard O'Brien and Tim Curry at the Royal Court, when I was about 15.

— Dawn French

You are a member of the British royal family. We are never tired, and we all love hospitals.

— Queen Mary

Contrary to the royal and uptight image of polo, I want to bring it to a younger generation. This is a great sport that can have a larger audience and appeal to more people. Sportsmanship is lacking in many other sports that I don't want to name.

— Randeep Hooda

If you ask me why I've succeeded, it's because I was in the Royal Marines. You have this unbelievable sense of achievement and of overcoming adversity. That's the confidence it breeds.
— Brian McDermott

There are no galley-slaves in the royal vessel of divine love - every man works his oar voluntarily!
— Saint Francis de Sales

Out in the lonely woods the jasmine burns Its fragrant lamps, and turns Into a royal court with green festoons The banks of dark lagoons.
— Henry Timrod

A plague on eminence! I hardly dare cross the street anymore without a convoy, and I am stared at wherever I go like an idiot member of a royal family or an animal in a zoo; and zoo animals have been known to die from stares.
— Igor Stravinsky

The Royal Family are not like you and me. They live in houses so big that you can walk round all day and never

need to meet your spouse. The Queen and Prince Philip have never shared a bedroom in their lives. They don't even have breakfast together.
— A. N. Wilson

I'm an officer in her Majesty's Royal New Zealand Navy. I'm a public relations officer in the Royal New Zealand Navy. Sounds good, doesn't it?—
— Mark Hadlow

We partied with the royal rich people, and we felt like rock stars. We drank all the whiskey in the place.
— Charles Kelley

Because of the earlier loss of the two elder siblings, my brother and I lived a very pampered and protected life. Nursemaids kept constant watch. With my parents busy at dinner parties and social events, we only met them as if for a daily royal audience.
— Charles K. Kao

Saudi Arabia has stability. The social contract and the political contract between the king and the rulers and the

royal family and the ruled people in Saudi Arabia is very strong and the bondage is so solid.
— Al-Waleed bin Talal

The Royal Family have always had an interest in a number of different areas of society. We are a part of society.
— Prince Andrew

Alongside my 'no email' policy, I resolve to make better use of the wonderful Royal Mail, and send letters and postcards to people. There is a huge pleasure in writing a letter, putting it in an envelope and sticking the stamp on it. And huge pleasure in receiving real letters, too.
— Tom Hodgkinson

Hats are the epitome of Englishness, and a royal wedding is the penultimate moment for a hat designer. I'm Irish, but I am a royalist and I believe in fantasy.
— Philip Treacy

When I graduated from high school, I had artistic and academic scholarships, and I was trying to figure out what to do. I decided to audition for the Royal Academy

of Dramatic Arts, Juilliard and the National Institute of Dramatic Arts in Sydney, Australia.
— Deborah Kara Unger

One of the few things in dance to match the Royal Ballet's curtain calls is the Royal Ballet's dancing.
— Clive Barnes

When the young Princesses Elizabeth and Margaret were growing up, that was at it's height and the War cemented that with photographs of the Royal Family having breakfast together and so on, by pinning their reputation so firmly on that particular issue.
— Anthony Holden

Neil Armstrong was no Christopher Columbus. In most respects, he was better. Unlike the famous fifteenth century seafarer, Armstrong knew where he landed. He also spent his time in public service, not in jail, and his passing was marked by world-wide encomiums. He ended his days as a celebrated explorer rather than a royal inconvenience.
— Seth Shostak

The royal road to a man's heart is to talk to him about the things he treasures most.
— Dale Carnegie

When I heard the royal family wanted to have me perform in celebration of — Prince William's marriage, I knew I had to give them a little something. 'Wet' is the perfect anthem for — Prince William or any playa to get the club smokin'.
— Snoop Dogg

When you look at Prince Charles, don't you think that someone in the Royal family knew someone in the Royal family?
— Robin Williams

When I was growing up, I did not exercise at all. I was raised in the French Quarter in New Orleans. If I saw someone running, I would call the police because I thought they stole something on Royal Street.
— Richard Simmons

Members of royal families are born into a world of indulgence and entitlement, and the princelings who grow up that way may never have to develop the emotional musculature that will allow them to show self-restraint.

— Jeffrey Kluger

The Royal Family doesn't go out shopping for their uniforms: they've got some guy sewing on all the ornaments in-house. You could say I've got my own in-house team as well.

— Theophilus London

One day, out of irritation, I said, you know all of those years with the Royal Shakespeare Company, all those years of playing kings and princes and speaking black verse, and bestriding the landscape of England was nothing but a preparation for sitting in the captain's chair of the Enterprise.

— Patrick Stewart

The colonies had little occasion to feel or to resent direct royal prerogative.

— Albert Bushnell Hart

My dad used to love Steely Dan, the Stones, Jethro Tull and all that. There was always Steely Dan going in my dad's car, but I remember The Royal Scam in particular because it has 'Kid Charlemagne' on it.
— St. Vincent

The BBC is the greatest broadcaster in the world. It's the standard that everyone measures themselves against. If we lose the BBC, it won't be quite as bad as losing the royal family, but an integral part of this country will have gone. But then, I'm an old guy.
— Terry Wogan

I would argue that television and particularly the BBC were instrumental in puffing up the Royal Family to a level where they were inflated out of all, all proportion to their relevance on the national scene.
— Andrew Morton

The Royal family have always been great philanthropists.
— Arpad Busson

The Royal Canadian Mounted Police and CSIS have provided extraordinary co-operation, as I mentioned earlier.

— Paul Cellucci

'Rapa Nui' is about the conflict in the 1600s on Easter Island. It's about the clash of the royal clan and the working class.

— Jason Scott Lee